Orlando

Merced

by Mark Stewart

ACKNOWLEDGMENTS
The editors wish to thank Orlando Merced for his cooperation in preparing this book.
Thanks also to Integrated Sports International for their assistance.

PHOTO CREDITS
All photos courtesy AP/Wide World Photos, Inc. except the following:

Louis A. Raynor/Sports Chrome – Cover, 6, 11, 15, 24 bottom left, 25 top left, 25 top right,
        28 top left, 30, 31, 40, 47 bottom right
Sports Chrome – 24 bottom right, 29, 46 bottom right
Buffalo Bisons – 4 bottom right, 47 top left
James P. McCoy/Buffalo Bisons – 5 bottom right, 15, 16
F. O. S. Inc. – 12, 46 top left
Michael Ponzinni/F. O. S. Inc. – 18, 25 bottom
Stephen Green/F. O. S. Inc – 28 bottom right, 39
Mark Stewart – 48

STAFF
Project Coordinator: John Sammis, Cronopio Publishing
Series Design Concept: The Sloan Group
Design and Electronic Page Makeup: Jaffe Enterprises, and
        Digital Communications Services, Inc.

LIBRARY OF CONGRESS CATALOGING-IN-PUBLICATION DATA
Stewart, Mark.
    Orlando Merced / by Mark Stewart.
        p. cm. – (Grolier all-pro biographies)
    Includes index.
    Summary: A brief biography of the versatile outfielder for the Pittsburgh Pirates who was an
All-Star in his rookie season in 1990.
        ISBN 0-516-20178-6 (lib. bdg.) – 0-516-26026-X (pbk.)
    1. Merced, Orlando Luis, 1966-   – Juvenile literature. 2. Baseball players—United States—
Biography—Juvenile literature. 3. Pittsburgh Pirates (Baseball team)—Juvenile literature.
[1. Merced, Orlando Luis, 1966-   . 2. Baseball players. 3. Puerto Ricans—Biography.]
I. Title. II. Series.
GV865.M398S84 1996
796.323'092—dc20
(B)   96-13994
                                                                                                    CIP
                                                                                                    AC

Grolier ALL-PRO Biographies™

Orlando

Merced

by
Mark Stewart

CHILDREN'S PRESS®
A Division of Grolier Publishing
New York • London • Hong Kong • Sydney
Danbury, Connecticut

Contents

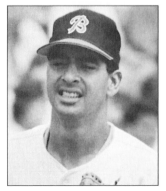

Who

Am I?

You probably think it would be incredible to live next door to your favorite baseball player. Well, I did . . . and it *was* incredible! What's even more incredible is that I grew up to play the same position—for the same major-league team—as he did! Sometimes I can't believe it myself. My name is Orlando Merced, and this is my story . . . "

"You probably think it would be incredible to live next door to your favorite baseball player."

Growing Up

O rlando Merced grew up like a lot of kids in Puerto Rico. He split his after-school time between the beach and the baseball diamond. His hero was Roberto Clemente, the island's greatest sports hero and its most admired citizen. Orlando was different from other kids in one important respect: he lived right next door to the Clemente family, and his best friends were Clemente's sons, Luis and Roberto Jr. Orlando remembers how their father encouraged all of the children in the town of Rio Pedras to play baseball . . . and how he would take his boys by the ear when he caught them out after dark!

Clemente was one of the biggest stars in the National League from 1955 to 1972. He spent his entire 18-year major-league career in a Pittsburgh Pirates uniform, winning four batting titles and starring in two World Series. Clemente was the National MVP in 1966, and he is regarded by many as the finest defensive right fielder in baseball history. "Unless you are from Puerto Rico, I don't know whether you can really understand what Roberto Clemente means to the people of our country. Even today, he is the biggest national hero in Puerto Rico. Every boy in Puerto Rico dreams about growing up to be the Pirates' right fielder like Roberto."

When Orlando was six years old, tremendous sadness swept through his neighborhood. On New Year's Eve, 1972, Roberto Clemente was killed in a plane crash. He had been trying to help the victims of a terrible earthquake in the Central

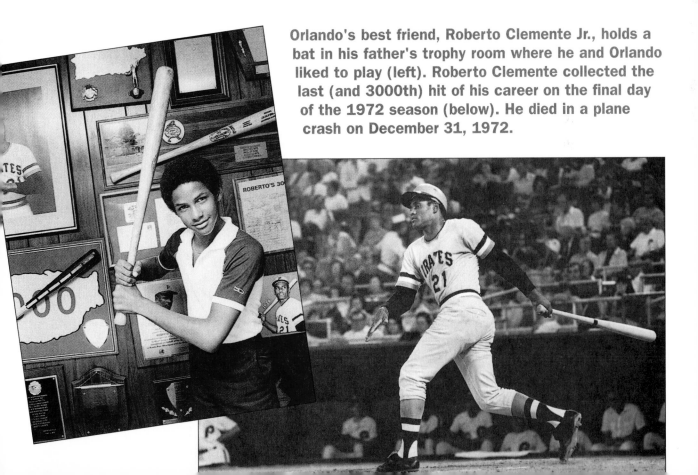

Orlando's best friend, Roberto Clemente Jr., holds a bat in his father's trophy room where he and Orlando liked to play (left). Roberto Clemente collected the last (and 3000th) hit of his career on the final day of the 1972 season (below). He died in a plane crash on December 31, 1972.

American nation of Nicaragua. Clemente had become very upset when he learned that supplies were not reaching the people who needed them most. Believing that the supplies would get through if he flew them there himself, Clemente decided to board an overloaded cargo plane headed for the devastated city of Managua. Something happened right after takeoff, and the aircraft plunged into the Caribbean Sea. There were no survivors.

Orlando, Luis, and Roberto Jr. all dreamed of becoming major leaguers. They pushed one another to improve, and they rooted for one another in games. They looked at the trophies and photos in the Clemente's basement and listened to Mrs. Clemente's stories of the hardships and highlights of her husband's life. It made them want to follow in his footsteps. Soon it became clear who the best athlete in the group would be: Orlando. He was good at almost every sport he tried, and the other children began to call him *Mayillo*, which in Spanish means "someone who does things better than everyone else."

Things did not come as easily for Orlando in the classroom. Although he was a good, hardworking student, he found certain subjects extremely difficult to understand. Math and science were always a problem for Orlando, so he approached them as if they were new sports he was trying to learn. He would keep working on a problem until he got it right. It took more time to do things this way, but Orlando did not like to walk away from a challenge. His favorite class was music. Orlando was a good dancer and played several instruments. Of course, he loved gym, too—not because he was the best athlete, but because he could try many different sports. Orlando also liked geography. It was interesting to see where Puerto Rico was in relation to other places he read about. And as he read about other countries and other people, he began to see how much fun reading itself could be.

"It is very important to read," Orlando says. "If you can't read, you can't survive in the world. You have to be able to read to drive a car, to learn about current events, and just to gain knowledge."

Orlando has been called *Mayillo*, which means someone who does things better than anybody else.

When Orlando enrolled at University Garden High School in the nearby city of San Juan, he wanted to play on as many sports teams as possible. And he did, becoming the star of the volleyball, basketball, and track squads. Orlando kept playing baseball, but quit the school team after his junior year. By then, he had his sights set on college. Playing sports for a living never really crossed his mind.

In February 1985, great news came from the Clemente home. The Pittsburgh Pirates had signed his friend Luis, and there was to be a big celebration. At the party, Orlando met Victor Luna, a family friend and Pirates scout they called "Uncle Victor." Victor agreed to arrange a tryout for Orlando. A few days later, Orlando was rocketing line drives all over a local baseball field, and Victor Luna signed him on the spot. The team gave Orlando a new glove, a pair of spikes, and a plane ticket to Florida, where he would join the minor-league Gulf Coast Pirates.

At bat, Orlando reminds many Pittsburgh fans of his hero, Roberto Clemente.

Road to

rlando Merced impressed the Pirates with his hitting from the moment he arrived in Florida in the spring of 1985. They also liked his versatility in the field. Orlando could play every infield and outfield position. What concerned the team was his size. He weighed just over 150 pounds. As the season wore on, Orlando wore down, and he ended up batting just .228 with one home run. This continued to be a problem for the next few years. Even though his batting skills kept developing, his lack of power held him back in the Pirates organization.

In the summer of 1989, Orlando was batting .240 with six home runs for Harrisburg of the Double-A Eastern League. In Pittsburgh, an injury to first baseman Sid Bream forced the Pirates to call up Jeff King from Triple-A Buffalo. This left a vacancy in Buffalo, and the Pittsburgh organization decided to let Orlando fill in until everything returned to normal. It was Orlando's big chance, and he knew it. In the final 35 games of the 1989 season, he collected 44 hits in 129 at bats for a .341

the Pros

In 1989, Orlando was promoted to the Triple-A Buffalo Bisons.

15

After gaining 25 pounds, Orlando started hitting with power. He even hit a home run completely out of Pilot Field in Buffalo (the X marks the spot where it landed in the parking lot).

average. Suddenly, the Pirates realized they had a special player on their hands.

That winter, Orlando was asked to start a weight-training program. When he showed up at spring training in 1990, no one recognized him. In a few short months, he had added 25 pounds of muscle! The line drives that used to drop in front of opposing outfielders were now crashing against the outfield wall. Orlando played the 1990 season in Buffalo and had a fine year. He even played a few games with the Pirates, pinch-hitting during three brief stays with the team.

In 1991, the Pirates were ready to challenge for the division title. The team was loaded with young superstars, such as Barry Bonds, Bobby Bonilla, Andy Van Slyke, and John

Barry Bonds (above) and Bobby Bonilla (right) were two young superstars on the late-1980s Pittsburgh Pirates.

Smiley. Gone from the team was first baseman Sid Bream, who had signed with the Atlanta Braves. Pittsburgh felt it needed veteran leadership at the position, so Gary Redus and Carmelo Martinez fought it out for the starting role in spring training. Orlando, the team felt, might be too young to stand up to the pressure of a pennant race. He was the final player cut in spring training. Orlando went back to Buffalo to start his seventh season as a minor leaguer. He began wondering what he had to do to convince the Pirates he was ready for the majors.

After being called up to Pittsburgh, Orlando quickly proved he could hit major-league pitching.

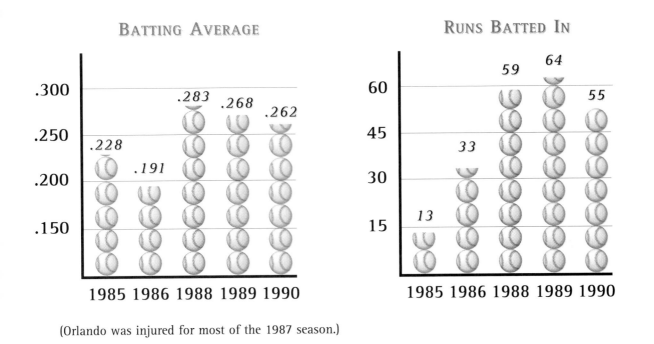

Orlando's minor-league stats show how he developed over the years:

BATTING AVERAGE

.300
.250
.200
.150

.228   .191   .283   .268   .262

1985 1986 1988 1989 1990

RUNS BATTED IN

60
45
30
15

13   33   59   64   55

1985 1986 1988 1989 1990

(Orlando was injured for most of the 1987 season.)

eanwhile, the Redus-Martinez experiment was not working in Pittsburgh. Both players had trouble hitting against right-handed pitchers, and neither was a good defensive player. After a few games, the Pirates decided that Orlando might be the answer. He had always hit right-handed pitchers well, and had proven he could hold his own in the field. The only question was if the young man would respond to being thrust into such an important position?

The Story

Orlando Merced was an impact player as soon as he joined the Pirates full-time in 1991. In fact, the Pirates might not have won the NL East in 1991 if not for Orlando. He stepped into his new role as a major-league first baseman as if he had been doing it all his life. In 120 games, Orlando clubbed 10 homers and collected 50 RBIs. His .275 batting average ranked third among major-league rookies, and the only National League rookie who hit for a higher average was Jeff Bagwell, who won the Rookie of the Year award.

Orlando did whatever the Pirates asked, including batting lead off when the team faced right-handed pitching. He showed remarkable patience at the plate for a first-year player, as pitchers tried to make him swing at bad pitches all season long. Only two other players in the league took a higher percentage of pitches in 1991, and only six had a better on-base percentage against righties than Orlando. During one eight-week stretch, he

Continues

Orlando's aggressive play has helped to make
him an impact player in the major leagues.

reached base in 35 straight starts. Orlando was not yet a complete player, but he was off to a fabulous start!

The 1992 season was a difficult one for Orlando. Although the Pirates won the division title again, he saw his average drop to .247. This is not unusual for second-year players. When rookies are successful, opposing pitchers often find new ways to get them out the following year. The mark of a good hitter is his ability to out-think the pitchers and regain the advantage. Orlando did show improvement—increasing his doubles, triples, and RBIs—but he had other things on his mind. His marriage was not a happy one, and he went through a painful divorce. He not only had to concentrate on his baseball career, he also had to worry about how his two children would react to the breakup.

As the 1993 season began, Orlando faced a new situation in Pittsburgh. The team's best player, Barry Bonds, signed with the San Francisco Giants, and the Pirates had decided to "rebuild." This meant that they would not be concentrating on winning, but on developing young players for the future.

As expected, the Pirates struggled that season—but not Orlando. Something magical happened that summer, as he played the best baseball of his life. Despite being shifted to right field, he was batting .362 going into the All-Star break. If he had not injured his wrist, he might have contended for the batting title that season. Still, he hit .313 and finished fourth in the league in on-base percentage. Orlando's increased patience at the plate resulted in a team-high 77 walks, and when he was able to work pitchers for a 3–1 count, he clobbered the ball for a .563 average. Since then, Orlando has established himself as a solid veteran. In 1995, he had his best season ever, leading the Pirates in slugging and finishing second in home runs and RBIs—a performance that Roberto Clemente himself would certainly have been proud of.

When he puts on the Pittsburgh uniform, Orlando thinks of Clemente. "Roberto is helping me from wherever he is. He pushes me to work harder. It's not that I feel I have the ability to come close to him. But there's a special feeling out there that makes me want to be as good as I can be."

In 1995, Orlando notched his second .300 season in the major leagues.

Timeline

1991: Finishes second in NL Rookie of the Year balloting

1992: Belts 28 doubles to help Pirates win second straight division title

1990: Makes major-league debut for Pittsburgh Pirates

1994:
Leads
Pirates
in RBIs

1993: Leads
NL outfielders
in double plays

1995: Leads
Pittsburgh
regulars with
.300 average

Game

Orlando's favorite position is outfielder, but he is also an excellent first baseman.

Action!

Orlando has played every position except pitcher during his time in the Pirates organization. He even played catcher in a major-league game!

Orlando's most satisfying moment was when he led off Game Three of the 1991 National League Championship Series with a home run off John Smoltz.

Orlando is one of the rare everyday players who can also be effective coming off the bench. In fact, he is one of baseball's very best pinch hitters.

Even though he's reached the majors, Orlando keeps practicing. "One of the things that keeps you working hard is the knowledge that there is always a younger player coming up who wants to take your job away."

In his first major-league at bat, Orlando lined a double and scored the go-ahead run in a win over the Phillies.

Orlando says "I'm very happy, but you've got to keep playing hard and you can't ever be satisfied."

Orlando has been a clutch hitter since his rookie season. In 1991, seven of his 10 homers either tied a game or put the Pirates ahead.

The first time I came up to the Pirates, I wore number 54. But John Hallahan, the team's equipment manager, took a liking to me. He told me that all the good major leaguers wore smaller numbers, and he gave me number 6 the following season. I wear that number in memory of John, who passed away."

"I started switch-hitting because I thought it would help me to get to the major leagues, and it did. I went back to hitting left-handed in 1993."

Dealing

Orlando is one of baseball's best first basemen, but he agreed to move to the outfield to help out the Pirates.

With It

Part of Pittsburgh's rebuilding program in 1993 was the promotion of a first baseman named Kevin Young. Orlando Merced was asked to switch positions and play outfield so that Young could get into the lineup. Some players would have resisted, but Orlando saw a chance to fulfill a lifelong dream.

"I realized I was going to be the right fielder for the Pittsburgh Pirates—just like Roberto Clemente!"

HOW DOES

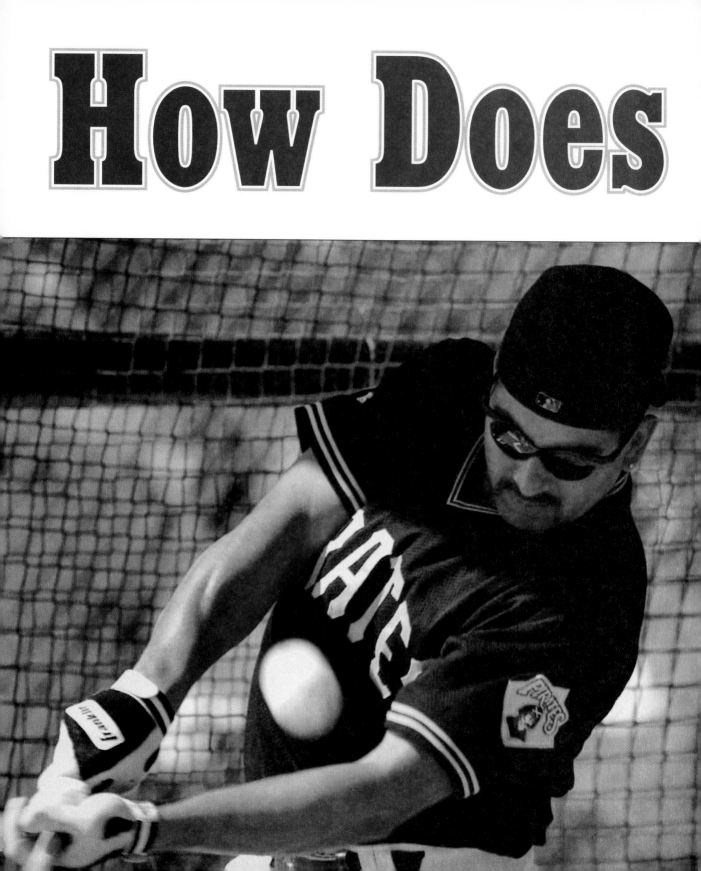

He Do It?

Orlando Merced became a true major-league hitter when he gained enough confidence to lay off "pitchers' pitches" and wait for a ball he could drive. That transition began in 1993, when he stopped swinging at breaking pitches he could not handle. He realized it was better to take a strike than to tap a weak grounder or pop the ball up.

"I am really proud of the improvements I have made on offense. And I still feel I am still improving every year."

Orlando's many hours of work in the batting cage has helped him become one of baseball's best hitters.

Family

Orlando has two children, Natalie and Orlando Jr. He spends as much time with them as he can during the off-season. Like Orlando, they love to play at the beach.

Orlando's father was a master sergeant in the U.S. Air Force, and then a mailman for 33 years. His mother was a teacher. The Merced family lived in Rio Pedras, a middle-class town outside of San Juan, the capital city of Puerto Rico. Orlando also considers Vera Clemente (Roberto Clemente's widow) and her children as part of his family.

"I owe a lot to the Clemente family," says Orlando.

Growing up, Orlando considered the Clementes (Roberto Jr., Luis, Ricky, and Vera) a part of his family. They still are today.

Matters

Say What?

Here's what baseball people are saying about Orlando Merced:

"He's really adjusted to playing right field . . . it might have something to do with Clemente being his idol."

—*Bill Virdon,*
Pittsburgh Pirates coach and
former Clemente teammate

"I talked to our scouts and they said he could hit . . . but it was beyond my wildest dreams how it worked out."

—*Jim Leyland,*
Pittsburgh Pirates manager

"I see him as a guy who can hit twenty home runs. He's got a nice stroke."

—*Terry Collins, Orlando's manager in the minor leagues*

"It usually takes a player three or four years to establish himself."

—*Ted Simmons, Pittsburgh Pirates general manager*

"He hasn't hit many home runs, but all of them have been bombs."

—*Tommy Sandt, Pittsburgh Pirates coach*

Career

The Pirates are looking to finish the decade the way they started it: with a mix of young, aggressive players and battle-tested veterans. Orlando Merced was one of those youngsters in the early 1990s. Now the team is counting on him to be a veteran leader. His credentials thus far have been impressive, but Orlando is looking to put up even bigger numbers in the years to come.

In 1991, Orlando was the runner-up to Jeff Bagwell in the NL Rookie of the Year voting. Cardinals star Ray Lankford finished third.

Orlando has already batted .300 twice in his career, the hallmark of a talented hitter.

Highlights

Orlando hit a home run in his first start of the 1991 National League Championship Series, leading off the game with a solo blast against the Braves' John Smoltz.

Orlando's strong, accurate arm enabled him to lead all NL outfielders in double plays in 1993.

In 1995, Orlando led the Pirates in hits, doubles, and on-base percentage.

Orlando quickly developed into one of the most patient hitters in the league. In 1993, he finished fourth in on-base percentage.

Orlando will go anywhere to make a defensive play.

Orlando's .300 average in 1995 was the best on the team. Carlos Garcia, who came up through the Pirate farm system with Orlando, finished a close second with a .294 mark.

Reaching

Orlando put his life on the line in 1993, despite a painful leg injury. Two of his friends had decided to take a motorboat for a spin one evening. They instructed Orlando to move his car and then meet them at a different location. When his friends did not show up, Orlando became concerned and went looking for them. He did not know it, but the boat's engine had stalled and they had jumped into Pittsburgh's Monongahela River in an attempt to pull the boat back to shore. When Orlando found his friends, they were in danger of drowning. He dived into the water with another friend and saved them. Luckily, Orlando had been a lifeguard back in Puerto Rico!

When it was announced that the 1994 All-Star Game would be played in Pittsburgh, Orlando Merced learned of a

Out

The Roberto Clemente
statue outside Three
Rivers Stadium.

project to erect a
statue of his idol,
Roberto Clemente, at the ballpark. Orlando
wrote to a number of his friends in the major leagues, asking for
donations to help fund the project. With his help, the dream
became a reality, and today the statue is there at Three Rivers
Stadium to be enjoyed by all.

"I did anything I could to help. Roberto's an idol to a lot
of people, and he created a dream for me."

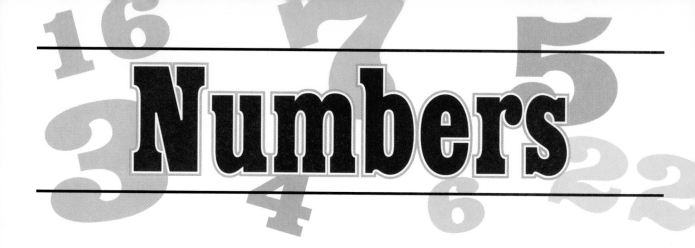

Numbers

Name: Orlando Luis Merced

Born: November 2, 1966

Height: 5' 11"

Weight: 190 pounds

Uniform Number: 6

Orlando's .313 batting average in 1993 was the highest for a Pittsburgh right fielder since Dave Parker won the NL batting title with a .334 mark in 1978.

Year	Team	Games	Runs	Home Runs	RBIs	Batting Average	Slugging Average
1990	Pittsburgh Pirates	25	3	0	0	.208	.250
1991	Pittsburgh Pirates	120	83	10	50	.275	.399
1992	Pittsburgh Pirates	134	50	6	60	.247	.385
1993	Pittsburgh Pirates	137	68	8	70	.313	.443
1994	Pittsburgh Pirates	108	48	9	51	.272	.412
1995	Pittsburgh Pirates	132	75	15	83	.300	.468
Totals		656	327	609	314	.292	.422

What If...

Right up until I signed my first professional contract, I was all set to go to college. I didn't get into baseball for the money, I just thought it was a good opportunity and luckily I have made the most of it. If I had not succeeded as a ballplayer, I would have continued with my college education. I'm not sure what I would have become, but if I could choose now, I would be a doctor. It's funny. When I was in school, science was one of the hardest subjects for me. But now I find it fascinating!"

Glossary

DEVASTATE destroy; demolish

PROMOTION the act of being raised to a higher position or rank

CONSISTENT remaining at the same level of ability; steady; unchanging

CREDENTIALS proof of having knowledge in a certain area, such as a diploma or a certificate

TRANSITION the passage from one stage, activity, or subject to another; change

VACANCY an unfilled position on a team; an opening

VERSATILE having the ability to excel in many different areas; multi-talented

PROSPECT someone who is looked upon with great hope for the future

RESIST to hold back; to oppose

STRIVE to devote serious effort and energy

THRUST to be forced into a course of action or position

Index

About The Author

Mark Stewart grew up in New York City in the 1960s and 1970s—when the Mets, Jets, and Knicks all had championship teams. As a child, Mark read everything about sports he could lay his hands on. Today, he is one of the busiest sportswriters around. Since 1990, he has written close to 500 sports stories for kids, including profiles on more than 200 athletes, past and present. A graduate of Duke University, Mark served as senior editor of *Racquet*, a national tennis magazine, and was managing editor of *Super News*, a sporting goods industry newspaper. He is the author of every Grolier All-Pro Biography.